One Above & One Below

One Above
& One Below

NEW POEMS

Erin Belieu

COPPER CANYON PRESS

Printed in the United States of America.

Grateful acknowledgment is made to Jordana Munk for the use of her painting on the cover.

Copper Canyon Press is in residence under the auspices of the Centrum Foundation at Fort Worden State Park in Port Townsend, Washington. Centrum sponsors artist residences, education workshops for Washington State students and teachers, blues, jazz, and fiddle tunes festivals, classical music performances, and The Port Townsend Writers Workshop.

LIBRARY OF CONGRESS CATALOGING-IN-PUBLICATION DATA

Belieu, Erin
One above & one below: poems / by Erin Belieu.
  p. cm.
ISBN 1-55659-144-6 (alk. paper)
1. City and town life – Great Plains – Poetry. 2. Landscape – Great Plains – Poetry. 3. Great Plains – Poetry. I. Title: One above and one below. II. Title.
PS3552.E479 O54 2000
811'.54 – DC21   99-050997
                                                       CIP

9 8 7 6 5 4 3 2 FIRST PRINTING

COPPER CANYON PRESS
Post Office Box 271
Port Townsend, Washington 98368
www.coppercanyonpress.org

for Jeremy

∽

*If the red grass were full of rattlers,
I was equal to them all.*

– Willa Cather, *My Ántonia*

ACKNOWLEDGMENTS

Grateful acknowledgment goes to the magazines in which many of these poems first appeared (sometimes in different versions): *The Atlantic Monthly, The Boston Book Review, Bostonia, Boulevard, Grand Street, The Kenyon Review, Lingo, Lit, Meridian, Nerve, The New York Times, Slate, TriQuarterly,* and *The Yale Review.*

Poems from the collection are also included in or forthcoming from: *American Poetry: The Next Generation* (Carnegie Mellon University Press), *The Bread Loaf Anthology of New American Poets* (The University Press of New England), *The KGB Bar Reader* (William Morrow and Company), and *The New Young American Poets* (Southern Illinois University Press).

"Choose Your Garden" is forthcoming in *The Best American Poetry 2000,* edited by Rita Dove (Scribner).

"On Being Fired Again" was originally commissioned by *The New York Times* for a poetry feature on the subject of Labor Day.

My thanks to the many friends who contributed to these poems: The One Fish Gang Collective (Mark Bibbins, Wendy Carlsen, Jeremy Countryman, James Kimbrell, and Ross Martin), Susan Aizenberg, Angela Ball, Kathy Fagan, Scott Hightower, David Lehman, Joe Osterhaus, Carl Phillips, Robert Pinsky, Alan Shapiro, and Greg Williamson.

I am very grateful to both The Rona Jaffe Foundation and to The St. Botolph Club for generous grants that allowed me time to work on these poems.

Contents

One Above & One Below

Timing Is Everything

– an invocation to the muse

Just as I've got him
going down, his soul tidy
as a presbyterian, the clean
bubble rising from his tongue,
that's when she says,

The drowned man
doesn't drown...

        The drowned man
doesn't drown?

She's like the gorgeous dykes
who rule my health-club locker room,
who own their skin like landlords,
with bodies beautiful as doom.

Her bare tolerance is palpable
and patchouli-scented.

        O sweet assassin
        of Mnemosyne,
        your kindness swings a tiny ax
        hung from a gold chain!

Poor character,
the drowned man who doesn't
drown. Bereft, a hunk of driftwood,
already growing pale, soft fish
gasping on her littered beach –

all he ever wanted was
to make a good impression.
I ask, *Is that so wrong?*

She ignores me.
She could finish us now.
She could unhook him
if she wanted to.

But she's busy
rubbing lotion in her fresh tattoo.

I

Your Character Is Your Destiny

        but I'm driving:
to where the prairie sulks
like an ex-husband, pissing
away his downtime in a day-old
shave, the permanent arrangement
this sky moved out on years ago.

You're in my jurisdiction,
the territory that makes old men
look older than their unpolished boots;
where only truckers get by, cranked
on speedballs and shooting up what passes
for an incline; where dead-eyed ranch
dogs drink oil from a roadside pool,

sick in the kind of viscous heat that will
fuck you without asking, and
whenever it feels the need.
You're straight out of my town's
post office, not the face on
the flyer but the blank propped up
behind him. You're the new stoplight,

the red direction from nowhere,
the signal I want to run.

Plainsong

He lived in a sod house,
a formal nest of grass
that wove green thread
around his soul, a bed
of mud and cellulose.

And she was small. She
never grew; the empty
wind that blew and reared
had bent her to the plains she cared
so little for. But he,

he didn't seem to mind
her size, he'd found
a shape to love there;
and she was spare where
he was generous as sand, the kind

of man who drifted
like the yellow hills that lifted
their sloping shoulders to the bad
lands. For her his mud
heart tumbled like the tufted

weeds that wheel along the plains,
that sea of mammoth bones,
that state all made of sky –
they married in July.
Her thin bouquet of corn

flowers remains the brightest thing
he'd ever see. I have her ring
now, a silver band so little
it won't budge over the knuckle
on my pinky. How long

ago, a man gave his grass
soul to her in her brown dress –
and she was always stern,
too small, and learned
to keep inside a sod house.

Wayward Girl

During their weekly outing, the girl drifts
around the Dairy Barn parking lot,
as the others adjust their plump
figures onto benches at a picnic table.

It is late summer and a dribble
of ice cream spots her maternity dress
where a pattern of washed-out daffodils
wants to decorate her belly.

A transistor radio fizzles out
Motown dance hits.
The girl bums a Pall Mall
off the take-out window boy.

She could be the official model for
generations of trouble, the daughter sent
away, to any place with parentheses,
which, in 1965, lay behind the gates of
the Salvation Army Home for Wayward

Girls. Euphemism suits the plains of her
imagined face, a Nordic face with angles
that conjure nothing more than snow,
deep snow. So her child is born

into trouble and expects to go out
unchanged, cursed with the urge to wander
all troublemakers carry, like a gene
soldered at conception:

in the back of a candy-red Corvair,
on the coat pile in any blue suburban bedroom
as the party music drifts down the hallway:

> *You don't own me,*
> *I'm not just one of your little toys.*
> *You don't own me,*
> *don't say I can't go with other boys...*

At St. Sulpice

Because the mind is forever building its model airplane:
locust hum of colored Bakelite,

blue lobelia in a hairy root-ball, plastic bags snapping
open, and unkind

comments up from Florida, or pearl-ribbed
radicchio, purple birthmarks lolling in their bin.

For instance, Delacroix's angel at St. Sulpice
is titian-haired like Nancy Drew, fearless girl detective,

which reminds you of *The* (solved) *Mystery
in the Golden Pavilion*

and wings, of course, wings, the angel's mashed
full-nelson in the foreground under Jacob's painted weight

in a church left suspiciously unvisited by tourists
except for two,

two scholars from the Hermitage resembling Cyd Charisse
and Peter Lorre, plus one bald German,

edelweiss, and Passchendaele.
Because the mind is forever building its model airplane

you have traveled off to Paris, saved up the fare
and expectations, have slept wonderfully uncomfortable

on strangely shaped pillows –
except

despite what you paid, everything resembles nothing
more than your hometown: Brigadoon

of perennial (almost eagerly) expected disappointments, as in
why have two scoops if one will do? And why have one,

etc., etc., Yours... sincerely, I don't believe in this
world sorrow, do you, Miss Honeychurch?

High Lonesome

Sick now for months, I wake
to the cold glaze of a night sweat,

a metabolic stone
tossed into a mossy river.

> The dream keeps me
> company,

faithful as a sunflower, the same
crenulated eye staring
from its chronic bed where
the moon greases the far wall.

In the dark, I hear the snow
counting to itself,
three mississippi, four mississippi...

> The dream listens, too,

old acquaintance,
paid nursemaid nodding in the corner,
the friend you no longer have
to speak with
> to make yourself known.

Welcome, genius loci, djinn fruit
weathering my salted field,

welcome home.

———

I am setting off with my father
in the cab of the 7 Up company truck,
his shotgun navigator,
working the route from Lisco to Lodgepole.

August smoked brown at the edges,
a dust-colored moth crushed
beneath the plate glass of the plains'
vaporous sky,
and I
am perched high on the black
bench seat, thighs pinking
against the burning
vinyl, the chrome radio knobs
in the shape of miniature crowns
too scalding to turn.

We're working the morning route
from Lisco to Lodgepole,

picking up the empties
for my grandfather, bringing the bottomless
box of stale candy bars and chewing gum
for the gas-station vending machines –
                                    and I smell the sugary,
acid stink rising
from the wood-slatted truck bed,
and hear the glass-rattle bell
the green bottles will make when
my father loads them,

the green, glass-rattle bell chattering
thirty miles back to Sidney.

———

Virus makes me plural, the whole
unveiled, an archipelago –

each organ cut off from the old continent,
new islands populated by marsupials
for whom we have no names.

Their ringed tails switch in the bloodstream.

———

My geography
      is defined by those places
      I was told never to go –

      by the lure of the train tracks
      stretched out next to the bottling plant,

where the brown bulls and rattlers
drape themselves along the hot rails,
listless, scorched ribbons,
their coils half-hidden in chin-high scrub.

      Not far away,
someone's aunt stands out
of the sun, hugging the shady rim
at the plant's front entry, below the old ad
for Kickapoo Joy Juice, the cartoon Indians
poxed where the paint has flecked away.

      Usually my father's
younger sister, not paying us any mind,

wearing her discontented face, diamond-
chip earrings, and a shiny summer dress
with quarter-sized spots of perspiration
daubed like perfume under each arm.

———

                              The reapers' house
was the only house
visible beyond the tracks,
where it leaned like a paper lantern
from a rise
in the unplowed field.
                    You could see the white tarps
laid out in a clearing beyond the front
porch, a cinder block pinning
each edge, the tarps smoothing over
the misshapen packages drying
stiffly below them.

Even then I understood their business –

even then I knew, everything is parts.

———

Now,
at the side of the highway, comes
the brown-haired girl
with her shoulder blades jutting
out like two pink wishbones,
the brown-haired girl carrying
the white plastic bucket, half-full, and
                              her father bending
over the bloated cow's carcass
down at the edge of the field,
its hard rubber belly hairless
and puckered like a dry lemon peel;
                              her father sawing
with his long-handled knife,
slipping it between
                    the fat and the skin –

———

Sometimes,
she appeared
on the old breezeway, a flock
of smaller kids
wandering out after her.

And sometimes
it was just her,
the brown-haired girl, her face
following the celebratory alarm
my cousins would make,
flinging handfuls of dust
as the iron rails began to mutter,
the train's pulse humming through us,
the measure for how soon
our freight would come.

Cephalophore

– for Dennis

Halfway up Montmartre,
the German woman props herself
on a portable chaise
and slips off her bikini top
below the Holy Virgin, who prays
from Her burbling fountain shrine.

French Boy Scouts shimmy
along Her edifice, vying
for an aerial view,
and I, too, hump up the hill,

the steepest hike in Paris,
where St. Denis first lost and then
acquired his higher, patronly purpose –

dead, he walked the city's length,
carrying his freshly severed
head like a martyr's receipt of sale.
Denis: one of the *cephalophore,*
a category of stubborn saints
who don't lie down until
they choose the grave.

Inside the church, the vaulted
chambers are terminally green,
snow-globed in shadowed dust. I pause
before a pile of melting votives –
squat offerings, anonymous
as organ donations –

and think we raise a host
of inadvertent corpses when
we name a child,
because you're here –

without my even calling,
you come: a boy, too smart, small,
astringent as a lemon,
your fine, wooden posture
already rigid, redolent

of dignity and persecution. You
who answered all questions honestly,
who stood foolishly
when you could have run.

In the flames' blue-bottomed
tongue, I see the three shack-trash

brothers who lived across our road,
how, one by one, they'd come
to beat your ass, as if
you were the task at hand.

And you,
standing fat-lipped, patient,
beneath the stunted ash tree
our father never could coax
to grow, facing your accusers,
who shouted, "Pussy!
Fag!" then raced back home.

But that's sentimental evidence
for your unlikely veneration –
if childhood misery made pilgrims
elect, we'd each have a congress
of apostles stumping at the Vatican.

Our mother says
she had no one in mind when
she filled in your birth certificate,
so I dump my pocketful of francs
into the tithing box with no request
for signs or miracles. Maybe just

a place in the spiritual
catalogs for partial incarnations,
for the image, struck clear
and cheap as a holy medal,

of a long-gone boy
not named for a distant saint,
and the consecrated style with which
he carried himself, searching for
the grave to take his suffering.

Radio Nebraska

If you can't be with the one you love, honey,
love the one you're with...

Good advice speaks from unlikely places, so you follow it
all along the Platte, heading west toward the panhandle,
the rumor of sandhill cranes fueling the tourist's urge,
caravans of birders cruising I-80 with a pilgrim's
progress. But what if you were born here,

and know this river's dawdle, its muddy elbows and
intentions? As a child, you had a child's frustration
with proceedings: twelve long times the hands must meet
before you reach the mountains. If you ever have a child,
remember to assure her that

one cannot really *die* of boredom, just an expression
folks use to pass the time, as one milo field drifts
into another and the same decrepit shed, year after
year, threatens to collapse. And isn't this the costume for
devotion? A sky so dense you wear the proof

of it, hostile actor in the packed cities your life is
pushing you through? An emptiness attached to
the spine like a vestigial tail? Broken Bow, Sidney, and

Alliance; Willa Cather's Red Cloud, and poor Beatrice,
her pure name made homely with the town's

local inflections. On your way through again, the cold air
puffing from the burned-out compressor barely keeps
the prairie heat at bay.

You've never seen the sandhill cranes,
but know the rites of their ethereal lovemaking.

    Otherworldly,
these alien birds, and unexpectedly beautiful.

I Can't Write a Poem about Class Rage

Too prosaic, didactic,
purely political, the cause lacking
a certain loftiness, unlike homelessness
or domestic abuse, those subjects
newly upholstered with the necessary,
American-style noblesse oblige.

Maybe if I were writing in
an Eastern European language with
a translator who caught all the verve
of my colloquial phrasing, writing
from a tradition that believes in options
other than the exhausted, ethical
tepidity of Art for Art's Sake,

the verbal icon spinning away
unsullied in some universal nook,
clean as Ol' Possum's toilet bowl,
that preatomic mode that's so *outre*
but keeps on spreading anyway,
then maybe I could get away with it.

But I can't write a poem about class rage.
Who likes to read about the real-
life troubles of the undistinguished poor,

a bunch of luckless, disinherited,
trailer-trash folk and their relentlessly
shitty lives? Even Keats, purged of his Cockney
accent, couldn't salvage a poem out of
my best friend's nephew, a kid too broke
to buy even half a billable hour, buried

away in the county lockup of some
unheard-of-by-their-own-standards
corner of Oklahoma, falsely accused
of raping an infant since the baby's
crank-addled mother had a score to settle
with the nephew's ex-wife. That won't
melt one stick of butter with
the versifying trust-fund crowd.

So I can't write a poem about class rage
without my own (no doubt) illicit motives
being called into question, and who am I
to take such a hectoring tone, to rant,
about someone else's baby or nephew,
and where are my credentials? What makes me
think I could throw a legislator's stone?

II

Choose Your Garden

When we decided on the Japanese,
forgoing the Victorian, its Hester
Prynne-ish air of hardly mastered urges,

I thought it would be peaceful.
I thought it would relax my nerves,

which these days curl like cheap gift wrap:
my hands spelling their obsessions, a nervous
tic, to wring the unspeakable from
a silent alphabet.

I thought it would be like heaven: stern,
very clean, virtuous and a little dull –

but we had to cross the bridge to enter
and in the crossing came upon a slaughter
of camellias, a velvet mass-decapitation
floating on the artificial lake,

where, beneath its placid surface, a school
of bloated goldfish frenzied, O-ing
their weightless urgency
with mouths too exact to bear:
      O My Beloved,

they said to the snowy
petals and to the pink petals soft as
wet fingers,
      O Benevolent Master,

they said, looking straight up at us
where we stood near the entrance, near
the teahouse half-hidden in a copse of ginkgo,

where even now, discreetly and behind
its paper windows, a woman sinks down
on all fours, having loosened the knot
at the waist of her robe.

The Possible Husband

hates these perpetual
Sundays, hates
the repetition of his waking
to the vague,
pink clouds idling
above his house.

He's home
right now, chasing
the last fruit around
his bowl of cereal.
He's folded
a paper towel
lengthwise, placed it
under his spoon.

The possible husband
keeps himself
busy, tells his married women
friends he's chosen
to focus on his work.
He no longer predicts
a relationship.

Late in the afternoon,
after phone calls,
after staking his tomatoes or
checking that noise
his clutch makes,

he will come in-
to his rooms
for the weekly visitation,
a parade of chimeras
who perch shoulder
to shoulder on his beige couch.

Their names are
so harmless they lift
like feathers from his tongue:
Susan, Lisa, Rebecca,
Amy, Claire, Danielle,
Sarah, or *Jane;* a furious
choir, they all speak at once,

and each has since come to
resemble the others, as if
his past were a police artist,

told simply, "Draw her grief
so I can see it. More like this,
and this... now, draw mine..."

K.

When your mother named you
she was brief.
One slender letter joined

at the center,
four stems reaching away.
She must have known you,

small and blue as nimbus,
would struggle with things
that weigh more.

She did you a favor.

In math books, K. is the symbol
for constant, yet how easily
algebra is fooled, confused

by the illusion of balance.
Better the weatherman
for you. He would call you

cumulus, offer a remedy
for the clouds, though your policy
scorns all conjurings and dire

prognostication. I'm glad
you weren't followed by N,
making you silent, or stalked

by the openmouthed A,
trapping you forever
in a corruptible tomb, waiting

out time with the Pharaohs,
stealing sound from the Phoenicians.

My Field Guide

I've never bothered with the names of flowers,
though now I'd like this expertise to call
them out to you as we hike in.

But I would want their true names, not
the guide's all-classifying explanations:

for *yellow simple-shaped* or *odd-belled purple cluster,* I'd rather plump-girl-
shaking-her-hair-out-in-the-shower,
and violet-prom-dress-circa-1960.

Or better yet, I'd have the words
that droning bee has just now written at
the throat of lakeside goldenrod. They must
be intimate – see how he calms between her?

His body, only evolution's hunt
for agitation, yet the way he gentles at
her feathered mouth. Let's call that... what?

Biology is obvious. Or choose
another name. No matter how you speak,
what language we might settle on,

the woodpecker won't stop her rhythmic knocking
inside the arms of tamarack,

and we've arrived at birds and bees again.
But nothing is as simple, is it?

On Being Fired Again

I've known the pleasures of being
fired at least eleven times –

most notably by Larry who found my snood
unsuitable, another time by Jack,
whom I was sleeping with. Poor attitude,
tardiness, a contagious lack
of team spirit; I have been unmotivated

squirting perfume onto little cards,
while stocking salad bars, when stripping
covers from romance novels, their heroines
slaving on the chain gang of obsessive love –

and always the same hard candy
of shame dissolving in my throat;

handing in my apron, returning the cash-
register key. And yet, how fine it feels,
the perversity of freedom which never signs
a rent check or explains anything to one's family.

I've arrived again, taking one more last
walk through another door, thinking "*I* am

what is wrong with America," while outside
in the emptied, post-rushhour street,

the sun slouches in a tulip tree and the sound
of a neighborhood pool floats up on the heat.

Against Writing about Children

When I think of the many people
who privately despise children,
I can't say I'm completely shocked,

having been one. I was not
exceptional, uncomfortable as that is
to admit, and most children are not

exceptional. The particulars of
cruelty, sizes Large and X-Large,
memory gnawing it like

a fat dog, are ordinary: Mean Miss
Smigelsky from the sixth grade;
the orthodontist who

slapped you for crying out. Children
frighten us, other people's and
our own. They reflect

the virused figures in which failure
began. We feel accosted by their
vulnerable natures. Each child turns

into a problematic ocean, a mirrored
body growing denser and more
difficult to navigate until

sunlight merely bounces
off the surface. They become impossible
to sound. Like us, but even weaker.

Dinner, After the Aquarium

When octopus arrived, I
was surprised again by the ways
we insist upon our metaphors.

                    An artful presentation,
the plate held all its charms, the pearly skin,
the bluish cups that hug the water's bottom,
curled open now as ripe anemones do. A curious
choice, I thought, for you.

You, too, have one eye sable in profile, though not
as soft, and also seem to glow cerulean
beneath the restaurant lights. The waiter offers
water and his undeciphered smile. You pass
on chopsticks, want a fork and knife to cut your dish.

I say, *The octopus seemed fatalistic...*
a languid resignation, the graceful braids
of arm and leg. I watch you chew – your tongue
slips up to whisk away a prick of sand itching at
your lip. I think about the drive to my apartment,

the cliché your palm will make
closing against my breast.

News of the War

The neighbor's wolfhound
is in heat again –

I hear her circling the block,
a shapely ghost that ruts
behind our garbage bin.

There is no fence
built high enough to keep her
home. The full stink
of summer leans on us

all; the poor and old expire,
sighing in their suffocating
rooms. I have come

to expect this, the small
event of her nightly
mission, tail held stiff,

divining rod that pulls
the storm, unleashing
thunderheads.

Francesca's Complaint

*Who will give me wings like a dove,
and I will fly and be at rest?*

Hell is not
what you expect –

    I hover;

above me the stunned
infants, the heathen's dignified
limbo;
       and below

where the circumference
whirls tighter and
tighter into
sin's essential funnel,

the eternal laundry
tumbles, washing the sadists,
the vengeful, veiled
in the frozen cauldron
        of Caina –

    At first,
    I was surprised –

When Minos lashed
the measure of his tail
twice around his body,

      I felt the blast,

reckoning
an awful impact,
the ground's apocalypse,

or worse, much
      worse, a kind of scalding

I could not begin
to comprehend –

such injury existing

      only in the arsenal
      imagination of God.

Our Father. He
Who Punishes,

like the household drudge
worrying the stains
set in a ruined sheet...

∽

Close your eyes.

There, floating behind the black window,

where the mind lives inside its glacier:

the clean, planetary light glowing
off its mirrored walls,

Whose is the first face?

Whose the ghost memory,
root the cold soul retains,

waiting in her waiting
room of wind and stars?

What does spirit, thread
knotted to the gristle
of a body,
                require?

A bone is made of something,
a vein, a heart –

                and who do they remember?

If I love
        the color of a melon's
                green belly –

If I want
        to scrape the bright pulp
                from its skin,

                to consider this
                        in my own mouth –

do you blame me?

How to love one

soul and not
another –

It is the art
I never figured.

I do not remember

a time when I did
not believe in duty –

       my mother's coin
       placed in my father's purse,
       my sin was, finally,

pride, for I knew
and was pleased by
all that had been paid
            for me –

and if,
on my wedding day,
those massive doors fastened

       as a figured lid stoppers
       the mouth of its urn;

if the church
cooled to a catacomb,

and the dust motes that baffled
in the little sun bleeding
through the great
altar window

> swirled grayly
> like a rain of ash –

do not call this a sign.

Hell is an honest temple,
> and love the amnesia

which allows me to forget
> nothing –

And this one,

who will never leave
    my side –

I do not say his name.

    (What better proof
    that He contains both
    the divine and diabolical?)

    The punishment for love
        is love:

Weeping has
undressed him,
while suffering mines
his beauty

as the silk digs
white and weightless
from the milkweed's

brittle husk –

and though the wind drives us
together,

we are not doves;

we never touch.

For I
am made the author
of this story –

I do not say his name.

The only sacrifice
He would take from me

is a broken spirit.

Lovely

Not the epithet
for an aging man,

like this man,

now climbing a staircase
into December light,
the sun lapsing

through him like a curator's
X ray unearthing
a recycled canvas,

the early figure loosened from
his body's ruined fresco –

but he is: Lovely,

sobriquet given for certain
girls sleepwalking their foggy
cusp, dozing the wet rim

of beauty's unconsciousness;

madrigal of contraries
containing both the clean bell
of birdsong and the bow's

dry tongue dragging
low along the cello's hip.

It's there in the join, where
a man's thigh meets
the ass's curve, raw as the rose's

puckered labia, his private
a cappella unfurling.

Mise-en-Scène

– the night ferry to Bainbridge Island

Despite the best efforts of
black-and-white,

this is not romantic –

Seattle backs up slowly, like a man
about to turn and break
into a run; commuters sleep across
fluorescent benches, the *tableau*
vivant of Red Cross disaster footage, and
she thinks of Miles Davis saying,

"The problem with American
women is they all want
to live in a movie." She'd laugh,

if the sound were not so mean-
spirited, so remarkably dark.
And who's to blame if
this night insists upon its stab
at film noir? He's no

Fred MacMurray –
no rabbit-eyed salesman, crushed
beneath the rubble of his cluelessness;

and as for femmes fatales, the vamp
drag and shoulder pads, that business
with the cigarettes, well, her hem's
unraveled, and she no longer has
the heart. But it's their movie,

so let's resist the urge to slap
on that cheap ending we've all been
secretly hoping for:

no sudden lifesaving conversions.
Those aren't blanks in her gun.

III

Brown Recluse

Spirit of the ratio
one above and one below,
she takes figures in a script
that haunts the cryptic willow.

Spoken in the dialect
known to every architect,
her cathedrals made of string
hold the stirring circumspect.

The web, a clock stitched from will,
chronologs which hours to kill;
when she rests, it's just a clause
in her gauzy codicil.

And when readying her bed,
she feels a pulse down the thread
current through the living weave,
she pins her sleeve to the dead.

Chest for Arrows

An educated schemer, will
of silver, six digits concealed
inside a doeskin glove – and yet
how gracious when they came to take
your head, the dark mass tucked into
a homely cap, *a little neck...*

Then history's a door,
with mirrors hanging on the other side.
And we, who squat before its keyhole,
might make mistakes, might see
exactly what we want to see.
(But wait – was *that* my self?)

A whore. A queen. A wife.
A doctor told me once that with
my orange hair, a dark mole rooted
at my left breast, I'd make a perfect
witch. There's one more strange figure
for the mirror, a body as

black art: what vanishes
inside of me, O Lord? And you,
Mistress of Schism, Nan Bullen,
bright thorn in Britain's parliament,

what would you say? A fact:
you introduced the fork to England.

What else? You wore your "gowns high-necked
to hide a goiter"? No. Instead you had
"a few moles, incident to the clearest
complexion." Whom would you believe?

I see you made a good end,
Christian before the French swordsman.
Your words composed, *a little neck...*

lie buried in a chest for arrows.

The Middle of the World

I wanted to dig there;
I believed I had been there before.

I knew exactly how it would look.

I knew a bare lightbulb hung from a string
from the middle of the world's ceiling;

that the place echoed pleasantly like a train station;

that the people I had known would be there, waiting.

∞

I asked my father for a shovel, and, when he wouldn't give
        me one,
walked up the street to Mrs. Gazantner, the tired lady who
        lived in
the brown house. She was sitting on her patio.

I asked her for a shovel.

She said   What do you want a shovel for?

I told her I was digging to the middle of the world.

She said   Oh. Well, ask Larry for it...

∞

I went inside the brown house where her son sat in the kitchen,
eating a hard-boiled egg in the gray light of white curtains,
and asked him for a shovel.

He said   What do you want a shovel for?

When I told him, he took me to the garage.

When I told him, Larry let me pick.

67

There You Are

- Togo, West Africa

Your cripple walks
up to the table pulling
his dead leg behind. It drags,

a branch of knuckles,
root grown
twisted from the socket.

You've been listening
to your dinner lose
its head. Behind you

the kitchen wall amplifies
a chicken's fear.
One nerve, how it

chatters. You're exhausted,
hungry; you know
the worst ways to leave:

slowly. A terrible
gift is a gift in a terrible
world. Your cripple is

a boy with only his nose
for an instrument, small
openings worked like

the stops in a piccolo.
He plays
"La Marseillaise,"

fingering the bridge
of his nose with surreal
expertise. You've just

arrived here, polis
of animated dust, already
you wear it in every orifice,

mud necklace sweat
drapes at your throat. Next,
your cripple plays "When

the Saints Go
Marching In" snorting
air through his nostrils, full

octave vibrato, human
kazoo. As the meal arrives
you pay for your

performance. You laughed,
then you didn't
laugh. Your cripple,

a boy (old accidents in
another country, green as wealth).
Steam idles a transparent

cloud, wet above your meat.

I Wake a Little Earlier Each Morning

to find the trees
are taking prisoners again.

You're certain that they're
harmless, benign as a flock

of founding fathers, the same
dignified postures, dropping

gnomish blossoms from
their black palms –

but the missing must go
somewhere when they leave

you. There's a flicker in
the atmosphere like a second-rate

spy with a pocket mirror,
and the trees,

the trees aren't talking,
they've got nothing to say.

You should get up early.
You should force them

to admit
what could be gone like that.

The Real Lives of Lovers

Aren't you tired
of the famous ones,

immortal in their ivy-covered graves?

Where's that infernal breeze,
or black plutonic love
embedded in a pomegranate seed
to plant your seasons in a row and spin
a captivating history?

How far away the past lives
from the present –

today you'd need a ball of string
to lead you back to passion.

Be like Wordsworth, then,
who claimed to find some recompense
inside his second fling with nature.
But who believes him? The middle-aged

Romantics PhD, who taught this poem
to you and countless rooms
of other glazed eighteen-year-olds,

did he shake his head a little? Sigh?
Who knew the torches he still carried?

Impenetrably beige with thinning hair
(though *Lamia* could light him like a grill) –
imagine what he once thought
he would die without. And you,

now standing from your desk to stretch,
shuffling to the back porch
for the evening's final cigarette,
the Pleiades above, those princesses,
embarrassing lesser stars,

what little bargains have you
failed to keep?

He must have been about
the age you are.

Nocturne: My Sister Life

I

Honeysuckles tap soil
    almost anywhere, junkyard
shrubs, able-rooted, attaching
    through rock or sand. From
Evanston to Omaha, their red fish
    roe berries border plots
of zoysia, buffalo, the family portion.
    Lilacs go slowly, their old-lady wigs
curling to beige crust; roses might
    develop, but die in extreme weather.
Depend on the honeysuckle
    to maintain where others falter...

II

You were never afraid of the dark, never afraid of each
object resolving itself, vanishing into night's good sleeve,
benign magic the world performed for you at sundown.
You admired the young shepherdess tending sheep at the
base of your lamp, coaxing her flock into evening's invisible
pen. You wanted the world quiet. Even then, you looked
forward to all things shutting their many mouths, interim
in the revolving puzzle of light.

III

Scent of an eighth-grader's
        cologne, they strong-arm other shrubs,
are used primarily for husbandry.
        Honeysuckles provide cheap
borders, hide chain-link fences.
        Won't tuck behind your ear, attract
bees bad as marigolds, and stand
        awkwardly in floral arrangements.
While not poisonous, the jellied
        berries can be semitoxic. Some
will not resist the urge to eat them,
        even after being warned against it...

IV

*Lying in your twin bed, where cartoon figures stare out
from the comforter with their medicated expressions, you
realize that you're dying, death includes you. Distant
relatives, rodents, and now, suddenly, you. This is the
same day you're surprised by a nest of wasps hidden in the
neighbors' swing set, their jet bodies burrowing inside your
clothes, stinging you between the shoulder blades, one welt
bubbling inside your lower lip. Imagine everything dead:*

your older brother, somewhere in the house, closer to it.
Your parents in the den, crunch of the ice bucket as your
father fixes his Manhattan (gold anesthesia, issued to the
heart), closer still.

V

When stands of honeysuckle
       fade, they reach for the ground,
their nippled flowers pulling close
       to the center of each bush.
Birds abandon old nests
       laid open inside the dying
grove. Eventually the shrubs
       must be stumped, hacked off
below the waist, and extracted.
       Do not be shocked by their roots,
how far the honeysuckles' reach is...

VI

Now you lie down queen-sized, new husband beside you,
paying rent in his dreams. Yesterday, he tells you, you
awoke with two questions: Needle? Needle? *Who knows,*
the way you sleep, you might as well be drowning. The

77

*dragonfly stuck in a knickknack's liquid glass. Sometimes
you drive a yellow Karmann Ghia through your dream-
scapes, clownmobile with transparent, cardboard windows.
Through shopping malls, bordellos, your cousins' basement,
you always ferry a passenger. Wake and something else is
waking: your familiar at the window, stalking what moves
on the ledge.*

Notes on the Poems

Written for Forrest and Susie Belieu.

AT ST. SULPICE

The poem's final line is taken from E.M. Forster's *A Room with a View.* The poem also makes reference to actors and characters in the 1957 Fred Astaire film *Silk Stockings.*

CEPHALOPHORE

St. Denis is the patron saint of France and his martyrdom is said to have taken place in Paris at what is now Montmartre (Martyrs Hill). *Cephalophore* means "head-carrier," and is the designated name for those martyrs who carry their heads to their places of burial.

RADIO NEBRASKA

In Nebraska, the name Beatrice is commonly pronounced with the stress on the second syllable.

THE POSSIBLE HUSBAND

Written for Don Lee.

K.

Written for Kay Auxier Horwath.

In ancient Egyptian, the word *ka* described the spirit that remained entombed with the body of the deceased. The letter *k* comes to the English language from the ancient Phoenician alphabet, in which an early version of the letter first began to be used around 1000 BC.

FRANCESCA'S COMPLAINT

The poem owes much to my readings of Robert Pinsky's translation, *The Inferno of Dante,* and to John Freccero's book of essays, *Dante: The Poetics of Conversion,* particularly his essay "Casella's Song: *Purgatorio* II, 112." Freccero suggests that Psalm 54 (Douay Version) is alluded to by Dante in *The Inferno* (Canto v, 82–84), and is a metaphorical foundation for the poet's theory of human desire. The poem's final couplet is a rephrasing of lines from Psalm 51 (Revised Standard Version): "The sacrifice acceptable to God is a broken spirit..."

MISE-EN-SCÈNE

Written for Michael Wiegers.

The poem makes reference to the 1944 film noir classic *Double Indemnity,* starring Fred MacMurray and Barbara Stanwyck.

CHEST FOR ARROWS

The poem includes details from the life and death of Anne Boleyn, Henry VIII's second wife, and the first he was to execute. The opening images refer to the popular rumor that Boleyn was a witch, though there is little evidence to suggest that she had the extra finger her detractors claimed as proof of her unnatural practices. "A little neck…" refers to Boleyn's comment upon hearing that a special swordsman from Calais had been sent for to perform her execution: "I heard say the executioner was very good, and I have a little neck." The quoted passages within the poem come from contemporaries' accounts of Boleyn's physical appearance. The title and final line of the poem refer to the historical details surrounding the disposal of her body: since no arrangements had been made for a proper burial, Boleyn's body and head were hastily buried in a weapons' case.

THERE YOU ARE

The poem was inspired by the opening chapter of George Packer's travel memoir *The Village of Waiting*.

NOCTURNE: MY SISTER LIFE

Written for Joseph Lease.

About the Author

Erin Belieu was born and raised in Nebraska. She received an MA in Creative Writing from Boston University and worked for several years as both the managing and poetry editor for *AGNI* magazine. Her first book, *Infanta* (Copper Canyon Press, 1995), was selected by Hayden Carruth for the National Poetry Series and was named one of the best books of poetry for 1995 by the National Book Critics' Circle and the *Washington Post Book World*. She has received awards for her poetry from both The St. Botolph Club and The Rona Jaffe Foundation and her poems have appeared in places such as *The New York Times, The Atlantic Monthly, Grand Street, TriQuarterly,* and *The Yale Review*. She presently lives in Gambier, Ohio and teaches English literature and creative writing at Kenyon College.

The Chinese character for poetry (*shih*) combines "word" and "temple."
It also serves as pressmark and raison d'être for Copper Canyon Press.

Founded in 1972, Copper Canyon Press remains dedicated to publishing
poetry exclusively, from Nobel laureates to new and emerging authors.
The Press thrives with the generous patronage of readers, writers,
booksellers, librarians, teachers, and students – everyone who shares
the conviction that poetry clarifies and deepens social and spiritual
awareness. We invite you to join this community of supporters.

For information and catalogs:

COPPER CANYON PRESS
Post Office Box 271, Port Townsend, Washington 98368
360/385-4925 • poetry@coppercanyonpress.org
www.coppercanyonpress.org

The interior is set in ITC Bodoni™
Twelve Book. ITC Bodoni was
designed by Sumner Stone, Jim
Parkinson, Holly Goldsmith, and
Janice Fishman in 1994 after research
into Bodoni's original steel punches.
Book design by Valerie Brewster,
Scribe Typography. Printed on
archival-quality Glatfelter Author's
Text at McNaughton & Gunn, Inc.